The Case for A Review of the Law of Murder

Foreword Sir Henry Brooke

MODERNISING Justice

Modernising Justice

ISBN 978-1-909976-38-2 (Paperback)
ISBN 978-1-910979-24-2 (EPUB ebook)
ISBN 978-1-910979-25-9 (Adobe ebook)

Copyright © 2018 This work is the copyright of Modernising Justice. All intellectual property and associated rights are hereby asserted and reserved by that organization in full compliance with UK, European and international law. No part of this pamphlet may be copied, reproduced, stored in any retrieval system or transmitted in any form or by any means, including in hard copy or at the internet, without the prior written permission of the publishers to whom all such rights have been assigned for such purposes worldwide.

Cataloguing-In-Publication Data
A catalogue record for this booklet can be obtained on request from the British Library.

Cover design © Waterside Press.

UK distributor Gardners Books, 1 Whittle Drive, Eastbourne, East Sussex, BN23 6QH.
Tel: +44 (0)1323 521777; sales@gardners.com; www.gardners.com

North American distributor Ingram Book Company, One Ingram Blvd, La Vergne, TN 37086, USA.
Tel: (+1) 615 793 5000; inquiry@ingramcontent.com

Printed by Lightning Source.

Published 2018 by
Waterside Press Ltd.
Sherfield Gables
Sherfield on Loddon
Hook, Hampshire
United Kingdom RG27 0JG

Telephone +44(0)1256 882250
E-mail enquiries@watersidepress.co.uk
Online catalogue WatersidePress.co.uk

Contents

Foreword v

The author of the Foreword vi

Introduction 7
- The Law Commission's 2006 report 8
- Changes in the jurisprudence on murder 9
- The present (2017) law 9

What is the law of murder?: A brief summary 10
- The law of murder 10
- Unlawful killing 10
- Any reasonable creature 10
- Under the Queen's Peace 11
- Malice aforethought 11
- The mandatory life sentence for murder 12
- Use of the whole-life tariff in England and Wales 13

What has happened since the Law Commission Report of 2006? 15
▶ *R v Jogee* 15
- Joint enterprise: The law changed by the judges 'because it was wrong' 15
- What is joint enterprise? 15
- Background 16
- The facts in *Jogee* 17
- Judgment 17
- Significance 19

▶ *R v Gnango* 21
- Inconsistency and confusion 21
- The facts in *Gnango* 22
- The judgment 22
- The public policy argument 24

- **▶ *Vinter and Others v The United Kingdom*** *25*
  - ▷ No legal bar to a whole-life tariff *25*
  - ▷ The facts of *Vinter and Others* *26*
  - ▷ Judicial history *27*
  - ▷ Argument before the Grand Chamber *27*
  - ▷ The Grand Chamber's finding *28*
  - ▷ Developments post-*Vinter* *29*
  - ▷ Summary of *Harkins v UK* (as it pertains to whole-life sentences) *30*
  - ▷ The continuing use of the whole-life sentence in England and Wales *32*
  - ▷ *Vinter*—'A misunderstanding of English law' in any event? *33*

Conclusion 35
  - ▷ Our views summarised *35*

About Modernising Justice 37

Appendix: Correspondence 38

Foreword

The *Modernising Justice* group possess a very clear understanding of how the criminal law operates in practice. In this short paper they are pressing for the appointment of an independent committee to conduct an authoritative review of the law of homicide.

What they are asking for is a rational consideration of the law in an area where politicians' concerns about a populist backlash have nearly always resulted in no changes being made—or even contemplated—with judges being expected to muddle along, using one fudge after another, to try and keep a leaky ship afloat. Two of the members of the group are former judges with vast experience of the way the criminal courts have had to cope in the absence of courageous political leadership.

I recall that when I was chair of the Law Commission more than 20 years ago the Lord Chancellor made it clear to me that his colleagues would not sanction a Law Commission study of the law of murder once our work on Involuntary Manslaughter was complete.

Ten years later the Commission was allowed to tiptoe into the area, but with restricted terms of reference. Sir Roger Toulson (as he then was) extended his term of office as chair by one year in order to complete its impressive report. Although it found that 'the law governing homicide in England and Wales is a rickety structure set upon shaky foundations', this report was left to wither on the vine for much the same reasons as had precluded any consideration of the topic in my time.

It is a British disease to prefer to muddle along without any concern about the consequences of maintaining laws whose quality cannot be defended on rational grounds. The Minister's letter on page 41 shows how policy is now being dictated by consideration of the uncertainty that is caused to victims' families when criminal law that was never fit for the purpose is belatedly corrected!

The dispassionate study which this paper calls for would pinpoint the parts of the law that cry out for change so that victims and their families never again have to suffer the uncertainties of which the Minister wrote.

The author of the Foreword

Sir Henry Brooke, CMG, PC was a former Court of Appeal judge, retiring as a Lord Justice of Appeal in 2006. He was chair of the Law Commission for three years from January 1993, the judge in charge of the modernisation of the English law courts from 2001 to 2004, and Vice-President of the Court of Appeal (Civil Division) from 2003 to 2006. He was a former chair of the Centre for Crime and Justice Studies. Sir Henry Brooke died on 30 January 2018 as this pamphlet was going to press. A tireless champion for access to justice and the rule of law, he will be greatly missed.

Introduction

1.1 It is over ten years since the Law Commission published its report on *Murder, Manslaughter and Infanticide*,[1] and the current landscape reveals no intention to review the law of murder further; either with a discussion of the elements of murder and its penalty, or analysis with comparable homicide offences, such as deaths under road traffic legislation. This paper discusses the scope of the 2006 Law Commission report and the relevant events that have occurred over the last decade.

1.2 The official view is that there is no prospect of any further legislation or discussion surrounding the law of homicide. The Lord Chancellor wrote to *Modernising Justice* on 31 October 2015 stating that 'the Government has no current plans to review the law on homicide'. In 2017 Sir Oliver Heald QC responded, on behalf of Liz Truss: 'I do not share the view that the law of homicide is in urgent need of reform'.[2] *Modernising Justice* is still awaiting a response from David Gauke. The purpose of this paper is to outline why we believe that the current official approach is flawed and out of step with current opinions of professionals who work within the legal, prison and courts system.

1.3 Contrary to popular belief, the whole-life sentence—also known as 'life without parole'—is a relatively recent phenomenon. The term 'whole-life' was first used by the Home Secretary (as he was then) Leon Brittan in a statement at a Tory party conference in 1983, and only appeared in legislation in 2003, in Schedule 21 of the Criminal Justice Act of that year.

1.4 'Whole-life' in the Criminal Justice Act 2003 appears in the context of orders and recommendations, and it can be used as a classification, but it is not strictly a sentence. Schedule 21 leaves intact the sentence of life imprisonment as formulated in section 269 of the Criminal Justice Act 2003. This life sentence relates to liberty, not to custody (a life sentence may be served partly on life licence).

---

1. Law Com No. 304 November 2006.
2. See Appendix: Correspondence.

1.5 To put the whole-life sentence in a European context, only the UK and The Netherlands have a whole-life sentence.

2. The Law Commission's 2006 report

2.1 The Law Commission, when it began work in 2003, was severely limited, with the terms of reference that their review should maintain the basic distinction between murder and manslaughter; it barred any review of the mandatory sentence of life imprisonment for murder. *Modernising Justice* will separately consider the penalty for murder in the context of overall policy, in particular taking into account the Law Commission's study on the codification of sentencing.[3]

2.2 The Law Commission Report advocated a reform of the law of murder, arguing for a re-categorisation of circumstances that result in the death of another person which are currently defined as murder into separate categories of greater or lesser severity. It also made suggestions for modification to the partial defences to murder, i.e. provocation and diminished responsibility. The recommendations of the Law Commission were well received by many and, as a consequence, a reformed partial defence of diminished responsibility was enacted in the Coroners and Justice Act 2009. In the same statute the common law defence of provocation (enacted in section 3 of the Homicide Act 1957) was replaced with a modern variant which is now called the partial defence of loss of self-control. The reform to diminished responsibility was almost entirely a reflection of contemporary opinion about the psychiatric treatment of mental illness. The Government did not accept the Law Commission's view that the opinion of the psychiatric profession supported the addition of a partial defence of diminution of human development, such that it could be available to children and young persons.

2.3 Other than these two statutory reforms and a study of the Offences Against the Person Act 1861, which was published in November 2015, no further action was taken by the Law Commission. The law of murder is therefore still uncodified and rests for its definition on the wording established by Sir Edward Coke 400 years ago, which we

---

3. For the current status of this, see http://www.lawcom.gov.uk/project/sentencing-code/.

set out in Section 5 below. In terms of the Law Commission's current programme, there is no mention of any future plans to reform the law of murder.[4]

3. Changes in the jurisprudence on murder

3.1 In the last decade a number of high profile cases have helped to shape the current law. They are as follows:

(a) A contemporary shift in the law on joint enterprise is illustrated by the decisions of the Supreme Court of the United Kingdom in *Gnango*[5]—and then *Jogee*.[6] Both of these cases are explained in Sections 12 to 21 below.

(b) The 2014 case of *R v McLoughlin, R v Newell*[7]—a five-judge decision of the Court of Appeal (Criminal Division) on the sentence of life imprisonment—is marginally relevant, although it misunderstands the judgment of the European Court of Human Rights in *Vinter and Others v United Kingdom*[8] on the violation of Article 3 of the European Convention (prohibition on torture and inhuman or degrading treatment or punishment).

4. The present (2017) law

4.1 There remains a significant body of professional opinion that supports the Law Commission's conclusion, in its final 2004 report *Partial Defences to Murder*, that the law of murder is 'a mess'.[9] Events of the last decade do not materially alter that mess, even given the two alterations to the partial defence noted above. It can hardly be said that the mess should remain unremedied.

---

4. *Reform of Offences against the Person*, Law Com No. 361 November 2015.
5. *R v Gnango* [2011] UKSC 59.
6. *R v Jogee* [2016] UKSC 8.
7. *R v McLoughlin, R v Newell* [2014] EWCA Crim 188.
8. *Vinter and Others v United Kingdom* App. Nos. 66069/09, 130/10 and 3896/10.
9. Law Com No. 290 August 2004, para 2.74 'The present law of murder in England and Wales is a mess. There is both a great need to review the law of murder and every reason to believe that a comprehensive consideration of the offence and the sentencing regime could yield rational and sensible conclusions about a number of issues'.

What is the law of murder?: A brief summary

5. The law of murder

5.1 The law of murder has been set out in the common law. It is defined as the unlawful killing of any reasonable creature by another under the Queen's peace, with malice aforethought.[10] The *actus reus* is the unlawful killing of a human being under the Queen's peace and the *mens rea* is the malice aforethought.

6. Unlawful killing

6.1 The unlawful killing can be by an act or omission. The latter can occur where a person has a duty to act, fails to do so and death occurs.

6.2 The words 'unlawful killing' exclude those killings in which the accused has complete and valid justifications in law resulting from self-defence or acting in the prevention of crime (so long as reasonable force is exercised).[11] Other killings are considered authorised for example during times of war. It should also be noted that the courts have made a distinction between the lawful withdrawal of treatment supporting life[12] and the unlawful active termination of a patient's life. The latter commonly involves what are frequently called mercy killings. The same can be said about voluntary euthanasia which cannot provide a defence to murder.[13]

7. Any reasonable creature

7.1 'Any reasonable creature' has been interpreted by the courts as meaning any human being not including a foetus in the womb[14] but is limited to one who is born alive

---

[10] Sir Edward Coke, *The Third Part of the Institutes of the Laws of England: Concerning High Treason, and Other Pleas of the Crown and Criminal Causes* (E & R Brooke, 1797) 47. In the original text Coke refers to the 'King's peace', however given the current monarch, we refer to the 'Queen's peace' throughout.

[11] Criminal Law Act 1967, section 3(1)-(2).

[12] *Airedale NHS Trust v Bland* [1993] 2 WLR 316.

[13] *R (Nicklinson) v Ministry of Justice* [2013] EWCA Civ 961, [2013] MHLO 65.

[14] *Attorney-General's Reference (No 3 of 1994)* [1998] AC 245.

when fully expelled from its mother's body[15] with an existence independent of its mother.

8. Under the Queen's Peace

8.1 It has been considered that the significance of this expression is unclear. In the past the expression 'under the Queen's peace' concerned matters of jurisdiction which is now provided by statute. In that now an accused can be tried for murder wherever committed if he or she is a British subject or, if not a British subject, the murder was committed within England and Wales.[16]

9. Malice aforethought

9.1 This *mens rea* requirement is satisfied by 1: an intention to kill; or 2: an intention to cause grievous bodily harm, i.e. serious bodily harm.[17] There is no requirement of ill-will nor premeditation.

9.2 Intention to kill or cause grievous bodily harm makes murder a crime of specific intent. There has been controversy as to how and when a jury should infer intention from foresight. Intention from foresight is an inference of intention made indirectly through foresight based on evidence that the offender intended or foresaw a result of his or her actions being a natural or probable consequence.[18] It should be noted that foresight of a virtual certainty may be evidence of intention,[19] or be equated with intention,[20] or a jury can *find* intention from foresight of consequences.[21] Making the test dependent on foresight can blur the distinction between manslaughter and

---

15. *R v Poulton* (1832) 5 C & P 329 (Central Criminal Court).
16. *R v Adebolajo & Anor* [2014] EWCA Crim 2779, Lord Thomas CJ, para 33.
17. Terms such as 'serious bodily harm' or 'serious injury' are frequently used, but for reasons of consistency we have kept to 'grievous bodily harm' (a term known to statute, the Offences Against the Person Act 1861 providing that intentionally causing (section 18) or inflicting (section 20) grievous bodily harm are offences in their own right).
18. Criminal Justice Act 1967, section 8.
19. *R v Moloney* [1985] AC 905.
20. *R v Matthews and Alleyne* [2003] EWCA Crim 192 (CA).
21. *R v Woollin* [1998] 4 All ER 103.

murder. In the case of *Hyam v DPP*, Lord Hailsham did 'not believe that knowledge or any degree of foresight is enough'.[22]

9.3 Grievous bodily harm is not restricted to harm likely to endanger life. Lord Edmund-Davies indicated that 'a person can be convicted of murder if death results from, say, his intentional breaking of another's arm, an action which, while undoubtedly involving the infliction of "really serious harm" and, as such, calling for severe punishment, would in most cases be unlikely to kill'.[23] The expression has also been construed as the natural and ordinary meaning of grievous bodily harm.[24]

9.4 Taking all of the above into consideration, the definition of murder simply put is the unlawful killing of a human being by another with the intention to kill or intention to cause grievous bodily harm.

10. The mandatory life sentence for murder

10.1 A person convicted of murder shall be sentenced to imprisonment for life.[25] As part of the sentencing exercise, all offenders convicted of murder are subject to a minimum term of imprisonment set by the judge, known as a tariff, the period to be served before he or she can be considered for parole.

10.2 For adults aged 21 (or in some instances those 18) and over there are four starting points:

(a) A whole-life order for exceptionally high seriousness: involving two or more victims with specified aggravating features, or murder of a child involving abduction, sexual or sadistic motivation, or murder for political, religious or ideological cause or a previous conviction for murder.

---

22. *Hyam v DPP* [1975] AC 55, page 65.
23. *R v Cunningham* [1982] AC 566.
24. *DPP v Smith* [1961] AC 290.
25. Murder (Abolition of Death Penalty) Act 1965, section 1.

(b) A minimum term of 30 years for particularly high seriousness which includes, but is not limited to, murder of a police or prison officer in the course of his or her duty or for gain such as robbery or burglary.

(c) A minimum term of 25 years if aged 18 or over and involving bringing a knife or other weapon (not including a firearm or explosive) to the scene with the intent to commit any offence or having it as a weapon and using that weapon to commit murder.

(d) A minimum term of 15 years if aged 18 or over at the date of the offence.

The court takes into consideration a list of aggravating and mitigating factors so as to consider whether to adopt a higher or lower tariff, i.e. number of years, than the prescribed starting point. It should be noted that intention to cause grievous bodily harm only is a mitigating factor.

Contextual Information: Number of Lifers and their Crimes

11. **Use of the whole-life tariff in England and Wales**

11.1 In the context of a prisoner population which exceeds 80,000 adults, the number of prisoners serving a whole-life tariff in England and Wales is very small.

11.2 The Ministry of Justice *Offender Management Statistics Quarterly* bulletin for England and Wales covering the period from January to March 2017 reported, 'The number of life sentenced prisoners (7,247) has decreased by 2% compared to 30 June 2016. There were 59 whole-life prisoners at the end of June 2017, with 4 additional life prisoners being treated in secure hospitals'.[26]

11.3 Those prisoners serving whole-life sentences have included some of the prison estate's most high profile offenders, often the focus of emotive press comment, such as Ian

---

26. *Offender Management Statistics Quarterly, England and Wales*, Ministry of Justice, https://www.gov.uk/government/uploads/system/uploads/attachment_data/file/633154/offender-managemen-statistics-bulletin_-q1-2017.pdf.

Brady, Myra Hindley, Harold Shipman (all three now deceased), Peter Sutcliffe and Rosemary West.

11.4 Public discussion of the whole-life tariff has in recent years been erroneously linked to Britain's membership of the European Union and a perceived loss of judicial discretion, subordinated to Europe. Whilst Britain's ratification of the European Convention on Human Rights is separate to its membership of the European Union, the elision of the two issues in the popular press and minds of the public obscures the reality of European jurisprudence in relation to the whole-life tariff.

What has happened since the Law Commission Report of 2006?

Through analysis of the following cases our aim is to highlight the inconsistencies in the law and its application:

(a) *R v Jogee* (Supreme Court, 2016);

(b) *R v Gnango* (Supreme Court, 2011);

(c) *Vinter and Others v United Kingdom* (European Court of Human Rights, 2013);

(d) *R v McLoughlin* (Court of Appeal, 2014); and

(e) *Harkins v UK* (European Court of Human Rights, 2017).

R v Jogee

12. Joint enterprise: The law changed by the judges 'because it was wrong'

12.1 In February 2016, the Supreme Court handed down a judgment returning the law on parasitic accessory liability (commonly known as 'joint enterprise', a broader term covering different types of secondary liability) to its pre-1984 position. In correcting the law in this area, the Justices of the Supreme Court amended a legal principle that has been applied by the courts for the last 30 years.

12.2 It is deeply troubling that so many homicide cases have been prosecuted for the last 30 years using an incorrect application of the law. This case is a key example of the need for review and reform of the law of murder in general; in how many other areas are defendants subject to a misunderstanding and misapplication of the law?

13. What is joint enterprise?

13.1 Although joint enterprise is generally understood to simply refer to a crime committed by two or more persons, its legal meaning is more nuanced and complex. Joint enterprise covers a number of different situations in which secondary liability can occur (that is, liability for a criminal act that was committed by one person who has been encouraged or assisted by a second).

13.2 The Court of Appeal has identified three sets of circumstances in which the joint enterprise doctrine could apply.[27] It is important to separate these out to understand the area of joint enterprise that is pertinent in *Jogee*:

(a) Where two or more people commit a single crime in circumstances where they are all joint principals;

(b) Where A assists or encourages B to commit a single crime; or

(c) Where A and B participate in one crime (X) and, in the course of this, B commits a second crime (Y). This type of joint enterprise is more accurately named 'parasitic accessory liability' and it is this type of secondary liability that was considered in *Jogee*.[28]

14. Background

14.1 The required mental element for parasitic accessory liability for a crime was set out by the Privy Council in *Chan Wing-Siu v The Queen* [1985] AC 168 and developed in later cases, including by the House of Lords in *R v Powell and R v English* [1999] 1 AC 1.

14.2 *Chan Wing-Siu* set out the following principle: if two people set out to commit crime A, and in the course of committing crime A one of them (the principal) commits crime B, the second person is guilty as an accessory to crime B if he or she had *foreseen the possibility that the principal might act as he or she did*. This foresight was sufficient to make the accessory criminally liable for crime B, whether or not he or she intended it.

---

27. *R v ABCD* [2010] EWCA Crim 1622, para 9.
28. Crown Prosecution Service Guidance on Joint Enterprise Charging Decisions (December 2012) https://www.cps.gov.uk/legal/assets/uploads/files/joint_enterprise.pdf

14.3 This had the illogical effect of requiring a lesser degree of fault to convict the accessory than that required to convict the principal. Whilst (for murder) the principal must have intended to kill or cause grievous bodily harm, the accessory merely needed to have foreseen that this was a possibility, without ever having intended it. This was patently unjust.

15. The facts in *Jogee*

15.1 The two appellants in this case, Jogee and Ruddock, were both convicted of murder by application of the principle set out in *Chan Wing-Siu*.

15.2 Jogee and his co-defendant, Hirsi, were convicted of the murder of a man called Fyfe. The co-defendants had spent the evening together drinking and taking drugs. Jogee entered Fyfe's partner's house, waved a knife around and said that they should 'shank' Fyfe. They left her house but told her they would return.

15.3 The co-defendants later returned to the house. Hirsi took a knife from the kitchen and stood in the doorway whilst Jogee stood outside, smashing a bottle on a car and encouraging Hirsi to do something to Fyfe. He came to the doorway and said he wanted to smash a bottle over Fyfe's head. Hirsi then stabbed Fyfe and he died of the wounds. Hirsi pleaded guilty to murder and Jogee was convicted of murder using the principle set out in *Chan Wing-Siu*.

16. Judgment

16.1 Following an in-depth analysis of the case law leading up to *Chan Wing-Siu*, the Supreme Court held that the Privy Council in 1984 took the law on an incorrect tangent and that it should be brought back to its pre-1984 position.

16.2 The court concluded that 'the introduction of the principle was based on an incomplete, and in some respects erroneous, reading of the previous case law, coupled with generalised and questionable policy arguments'.

16.3 The court recognised the significance of reversing this statement of principle, setting out several reasons for doing so:

(a) The court had the benefit of a fuller analysis of the relevant case law than on previous occasions.

(b) The law was not well-established and had not been working satisfactorily. It was difficult for trial judges to apply and led to many appeals.

(c) If a wrong turn had been taken in such an important part of the common law, it must be corrected. As this principle had always been part of common law and not statute, it was correct for the courts to rectify it.

(d) In common law, foresight is simply evidence of the requisite intention (albeit strong evidence). Given that murder already has a low fault threshold (the defendant need not have intended to kill, but only to cause grievous bodily harm), the lesser degree of culpability required for the accessory by the *Chan Wing-Siu* principle was an over-extension of the law of murder.

(e) The *Chan Wing-Siu* principle was anomalous insofar as it required a lower mental threshold for guilt in the case of the accessory than the principal.

16.4 The court then acknowledged that it must set out clearly the relevant principles going forward.

16.5 In doing so, it re-stated that the earlier error was to *equate foresight with intent*. What matters is not foresight but *whether the accessory encouraged or assisted the crime*. If the crime is murder, the required fault of the accessory is intention to assist the principal to intentionally cause (at least) grievous bodily harm.

16.6 Finally, the court explicitly dealt with the impact of its decision on past convictions. Although an important statement of principle, it did not necessarily affect the outcome of many previous convictions. As past convictions were handed down on the law as it stood at the time, appeals could only now be allowed with exceptional leave to appeal out of time. The Court of Appeal would not allow such appeals simply because the law at the time had now been found to have been mistaken. In addition, this change in principle did not mean that all defendants convicted under the previous principle would now be found not guilty. Indeed, foresight is very strong evidence of the requisite intention to assist.

17. Significance

17.1 Jogee and Ruddock were entitled to have their appeals considered as they were brought in time. The court considered that Jogee was without doubt guilty of manslaughter at least and rejected counsel's submissions that he be found not guilty of murder or manslaughter. Jogee will now face trial again under the new legal principle.

17.2 This judgment has been widely reported in the press and caused a significant stir amongst the public, fuelled by headlines suggesting that dozens of murderers would now have their convictions overturned and 'walk free'.

17.3 It is cases such as this, and the (mis)reporting of them in the media, that demonstrate why it is so difficult to gather public support to lobby for reform of the law of murder. The nuances of judgments and their effects upon individual cases are rarely accurately captured by a newspaper headline. In this instance, the court expressly stated in its judgment its limited application to past convictions.

17.4 The law in this area was initially developed to cover cases where it was unknown or unclear which defendant had been the one to physically commit the criminal act. The campaign group Joint Enterprise Not Guilty by Association (JENGbA), an intervener in this case, has been campaigning 'to reform legal abuse by Joint Enterprise' since 2010.[29] They highlight that the principle has actually been expanded so as to become a policy decision to expand the law of murder far beyond its original boundaries. They point out that people have been charged under this principle when they have simply been in the vicinity of a crime or had a connection to the perpetrator, even via a phone call.

17.5 One of JENGbA's cases concerns Jordan Cunliffe, who was convicted of murder by joint enterprise after being present at an unplanned attack where two of his friends

---

29. See http://www.jointenterprise.co/default.html

struck a fatal blow to Gary Newlove.[30] Cunliffe was a few yards away from the incident and suffers from a degenerative eye condition which meant that he would not have had a clear view of the attack.

17.6 Just for Kids Law, another intervener in the case, argued that the principle has been used to disproportionately convict young black men of serious crimes.[31] A study by Dr Ben Crewe and colleagues from Cambridge University Institute of Criminology found that 37 per cent of joint enterprise prisoners were black, compared to 12 per cent of prisoners in the general prison population.[32]

17.7 Although the Criminal Cases Review Commission (CCRC) may receive an influx of applications following *Jogee*, the Supreme Court anticipated that it will only affect a small number of cases in very specific circumstances. However, Mark George QC has written an interesting commentary in relation to the court's opinion on this point. He argues that *Jogee* has not changed the law; it has simply clarified it. He therefore challenges the part of the judgment in *Jogee* that states that appeals will not be heard simply because the law as then applied has now been found to be mistaken. He argues that although the *interpretation* of the law changed, the law itself did not. This is not an instance where government has amended/enacted an Act of Parliament that would have changed the outcome of a decision if in force at the relevant time.[33] Mark George criticises the judgment for giving the CCRC another reason to refuse to refer cases to the Court of Appeal.[34]

17.8 It remains to be seen how the judgment in *Jogee* will affect those currently sentenced under joint enterprise law and how the CCRC will deal with applications for leave to appeal. Mark George's commentary suggests that this may not be simple.

---

30. *R (On the application of Cunliffe) v Secretary of State for Justice* [2016] EWHC 984 (Admin).
31. See statement from Just for Kids Law following the decision in *R v Jogee:* http://www.justforkidslaw.org/news-events/statement-from-just-for-kids-law-following-supreme-court-judgment-in-jogee
32. Ibid; see also the submission of Dr Ben Crewe, Dr Susie Hulley and Ms Serena Wright, Institute of Criminology, University of Cambridge: http://www.crim.cam.ac.uk/research/ltp_from_young_adulthood/evidence_to_justice_committee.pdf
33. Mark George QC, 'Fresh Appeals After R v Jogee'. https://mmchgeorge99.wordpress.com/2016/02/24/fresh-appeals-after-r-v-jogee/.
34. Ibid.

17.9 Under current sentencing laws, once the accessory has been convicted of murder, he or she must be given a life sentence despite not having committed the lethal act (and in some cases not intended it either). This case is a shining example of the need for more general reform of the law of murder. If the way the law of homicide has been functioning in this particular area for the last 30 years is incorrect, it is surely time for the courts and Parliament to examine the law on homicide more widely and ensure that it is clear, just and fairly applied.

R v Gnango

18. Inconsistency and confusion

18.1 *R v Gnango* is a case that was heard in 2011 — five years prior to *Jogee*. The facts are presented below, however detailed analysis of this case presents a strong argument for the reform of the law of murder. The inconsistencies presented by it are stark and the confusion that followed evident. It was hoped and anticipated that the Supreme Court would use this case as an opportunity to demystify the law surrounding parasitic accessory liability. However the outcome of the judgment offered more confusion than clarity. In fact what the judgment in *Gnango* presents is an inability by the judges 'to present a clear account of why Gnango was a murderer'.[35]

18.2 It could be argued that following *Jogee* further consideration of this case is no longer necessary. However it would be contended that the judgment in *Gnango* should not be ignored following the success in *Jogee* to clarify the law and principles surrounding parasitic accessory liability. *Gnango* is in fact a stark reminder of the worrying state of the law of murder in this country. It is vitally important to consider why the highest court in the land was unable to reach a sound conclusive judgment for others to follow.

---

35. Findlay Stark, '"A Most Difficult Case": On the *Ratio* of *Gnango*' (2013), *Cambridge Journal of International and Comparative Law*, 60 at 62.

19. The facts in *Gnango*

19.1 On the evening of Tuesday 2 October 2007, a 26-year-old polish care worker, Magda Pniewska, was walking home from work. Her route took her through a car park for residential accommodation in New Cross, South London. As she walked up a set of stairs whilst on the telephone to her sister, a single bullet wound to her head killed her. The bullet was fired as a result of a shootout between two young males.

19.2 Gnango had had an earlier altercation with another young male, who is known as Bandana Man. Gnango visited the house of his ex-girlfriend with another friend and then he and that friend drove to a car park elsewhere on the same estate. Gnango then left the car and walked to another car park close by. Gnango was armed with a gun.

19.3 As Gnango arrived at the nearby car park, there was a red car, a Volkswagen Polo, already parked. He approached the car and spoke to the occupants of which there were four. In that conversation Gnango is reported to have said, 'He had come to meet someone to handle some business'. Gnango asked the occupants if they had seen a man in a red bandana explaining that this man owed him some money.

19.4 The occupants in the red Polo then saw an individual wearing a red bandana come down the steps towards the car park. Bandana Man then pulled out a gun and began shooting at Gnango. Gnango crouched behind the Polo and returned fire. The occupants gave evidence that Gnango was firing shots at Bandana Man.

19.5 In the crossfire between Gnango and Bandana Man, Ms Pniewska was killed. It was proved that the fatal shot came from Bandana Man's gun and not from Gnango's weapon. Bandana Man and Gnango fled the scene. Bandana Man was never charged. *Prima facie*, he would be liable for the murder of Ms Pniewska under the historic common law doctrine of transferred malice, i.e. if intending to kill or cause serious harm to Gnango he killed a third party. Gnango was arrested four days after the crime.

20. The judgment

20.1 The question before the Supreme Court, and the consideration upon which the appeal was granted, was:

'If (1) D1 and D2 voluntarily engage in fighting each other, each intending to kill or cause grievous bodily harm to the other and each foreseeing that the other has the reciprocal intention, and if (2) D1 mistakenly kills V in the course of the fight, in what circumstances, if any, is D2 guilty of the offence of murdering V?'[36]

20.2 The Supreme Court Justices noted that there was no previous decision that would provide 'a clear indication of how the point of law should be resolved.'[37] It was therefore an opportunity for them to collectively demonstrate and restate the relevant principles. However there was no continuity of approach by the judges making it particularly difficult to work out what the ratio of *Gnango* actually is.[38] The only continuity being that for differing reasons the judges found that parasitic accessory liability was not a sound basis for conviction in this case.

20.3 In a joint judgment, Lord Phillips and Lord Judge found that Gnango had been properly convicted at first instance. Both judges found that Gnango 'aided and abetted the commission of the murder by actively encouraging Bandana Man to shoot at him'.[39] Gnango was therefore an accessory to his own attempted murder by virtue of the fact he had encouraged Bandana Man to shoot at him whilst having the foresight that Bandana Man would retaliate and continue firing at Gnango with the intention of killing him. Lord Wilson also agreed with this judgment.

20.4 Lord Brown and Lord Clarke however considered this case to be 'one of primary, rather than secondary liability'.[40] For both, Gnango was liable for the murder of Ms Pniewska as a principal — 'a direct participant engaged by agreement in unlawful violence specifically designed to cause death'.[41] The facts of Gnango's case were likened to that of an old-fashioned duel. Lord Brown made clear that 'by engaging

---

36. *R v Gnango* [2011] UKSC 59, para 1.
37. Ibid, para 2.
38. Findlay Stark, '"A Most Difficult Case": On the *Ratio* of *Gnango*' (2013), *Cambridge Journal of International and Comparative Law*, 60 at 62.
39. *R v Gnango* [2011] UKSC 59, para 46.
40. Findlay Stark, '"A Most Difficult Case": On the *Ratio* of *Gnango*' (2013), *Cambridge Journal of International and Comparative Law*, 60 at 63.
41. R Craig Connal QC, 'The Escape of Bandana Man: Guilty of Not Firing the Fatal Bullet' (2012), *Judicial Review*, 305 at 310.

in gunfire Mr Gnango became directly and primarily liable for the fact that another person engaging in gunfire with him shot a bystander'.[42]

20.5 By contrast, Lord Phillips and Lord Judge considered that in the context of this particular case the distinction between primary and secondary liability was in fact 'immaterial'.[43] They concluded that: 'Whether, on strict analysis, that made [Mr Gnango] guilty as a principal to Bandana Man's *actus reus* of firing the fatal shot, or guilty as one who had "aided, abetted counselled or procured" his firing of that shot creates no practical difficulty … and does not affect the result'.

20.6 Lord Kerr, the sole dissenting voice, understandably accepted that Ms Pniewska's death was an 'appalling tragedy'.[44] However he appeared unswayed by the 'public policy grounds strongly weighted in favour of upholding'[45] Gnango's conviction and instead quashed it. Lord Kerr did not find evidence to uphold it as the other judges had, based on the arguments of Gnango's primary or secondary liability.

21. The public policy argument

21.1 As Professor Graham Virgo so accurately describes it 'at the heart of their judgments is the assumption that Gnango should be convicted of murder, for that is what the public would expect'.[46] Lord Brown and Lord Clarke in particular were not shy to state honestly the public policy position on which their judgments were based. Lord Brown felt strongly that the public would be 'astonished and appalled' if the conviction had not been upheld. However, it must be honestly questioned whether the public opinion in favour of conviction 'is a more appropriate guide here than is

---

42. Ibid.
43. Findlay Stark, '"A Most Difficult Case": On the *Ratio* of *Gnango*' (2013), *Cambridge Journal of International and Comparative Law*, 60 at 63. See also *R v Gnango* [2011] UKSC 59, para 27.
44. *R v Gnango* [2011] UKSC 59, para 64.
45. R Craig Connal QC, 'The Escape of Bandana Man: Guilty of Not Firing the Fatal Bullet' (2012) *Judical Review*, 305 at 312.
46. Professor Graham Virgo, 'Guilt by Association: A Reply to Peter Mirfield' (2013), *Criminal Law Review*, Issue 7, 584.

judicial common sense'.[47] It is a concerning position to be in when the law is being used as a tool to convict an individual because that is what the general public would want and expect. One would question if this is just application of the law or simply mob mentality.

21.2   Peter Mirfield poses a very interesting question — had Bandana Man been caught and convicted would the legal community have still conceived that Gnango be charged with murder? If the answer to that question would be no, we are in danger of inconsistent and unfair application of the law in this unusual case. It would be contended 'a fixation on the "right" result led to a lack of concern for the route taken towards it'.[48]

21.3   The law of murder is currently enveloped in confusion, myth and misunderstanding. It is a contentious area of the law that politicians are scared to approach, in fear of damaging their chances of re-election. However, it is imperative that such a review is conducted to avoid further misapplication of the law of murder to construct convictions where the public outcry calls for it. In our view *Gnango* is a useful tool to demonstrate that the complexities of modern-day society are often better served by the certainties and precision of statute. It would appear to many that justice has been served through the judgment in *Gnango*. However, one would question whether the judgment has been reached by legitimate means.

Vinter and Others v The United Kingdom

22.   No legal bar to a whole-life tariff

22.1   The case of *Vinter and Others v The United Kingdom* App. Nos. 66069/09, 130/10 and 3896/10 (ECHR, 9 July 2013) was heard by the Grand Chamber of the European Court of Human Rights in 2013.

---

47.   Peter Mirfield, 'Guilt by Association: A Reply to Professor Virgo' (2013), *Criminal Law Review*, Issue 7, 577 at 583.

48.   Findlay Stark, "A Most Difficult Case": On the *Ratio* of *Gnango*' (2013), *Cambridge Journal of International and Comparative Law*, 60 at 66.

22.2   The judgment of the Grand Chamber offered clarification on the situations in which whole-life tariffs are a breach of Article 3 of the European Convention on Human Rights. The case shows that the UK government may continue to make statutory provision for whole-life tariffs but only where the sentence includes established review dates. The point in the sentence at which such reviews must be made was not stated by the court and the UK Government's stance has been to narrow down prisoners' rights to review as far as legally possible.

23. The facts of *Vinter and Others*

23.1   *Vinter* concerned three applicants, each of whom was incarcerated under a whole-life tariff in England. The first applicant, Vinter, had his whole-life tariff set by a trial judge in 2008. The second and third applicants, Bamber and Moore respectively, had their whole-life tariffs set by the Secretary of State under the pre-existing system, i.e. these two tariffs were imposed prior to the commencement of the Criminal Justice Act 2003 which transferred responsibility to the judiciary and laid down statutory criteria for whole-life tariffs in Schedule 21 of that Act.

23.2   Prior to 2003, the Secretary of State (the Home Secretary) was able to review the sentences of prisoners serving a whole-life tariff after 25 years, at which point he or she would decide whether incarceration was still necessary. When the Criminal Justice Act 2003 was enacted, this power was removed from the Secretary of State and instead placed in the hands of High Court judges.

23.3   The second and third applicants asked for their tariffs to be reviewed by the High Court after the commencement of the 2003 Act. These reviews did not result in a reduction of the sentence tariffs.

23.4   The first applicant also had his sentence and tariff reviewed on appeal to the Court of Appeal. However, the court did not depart from the principle in Schedule 21 to the 2003 Act that a murder committed by someone who had previously been convicted of murder should receive a whole-life tariff.

23.5 All the applicants argued that a whole-life tariff is contrary to Article 3 of the European Convention on Human Rights (prohibition on torture or inhuman or degrading treatment or punishment).

24. Judicial history

24.1 Initially, the applicants' appeal to the European Court of Human Rights was heard by a chamber of seven judges. The chamber held by a 4–3 majority that, although it is rare to find the whole-life tariff in the statutory regimes of other member states, it does not breach Article 3. Only the minority held that lack of a sentence review date leads to a breach of Article 3.

24.2 Subsequently, the applicants appealed to the Grand Chamber for a review of the chamber's judgment at the first applicant's request.

25. Argument before the Grand Chamber

25.1 Before the Grand Chamber the UK Government argued that the penal policy in England and Wales is long-standing, well-established and reflects the view — both of the domestic courts and Parliament — that some crimes warrant lifelong incarceration for the purpose of punishment due to their grievousness. The case took place in the context of agreement between the parties that a life sentence without the possibility of parole was, in principle, incompatible with Article 3.

25.2 The Government further submitted that the chamber had been correct to find that a discretionary life sentence with a whole-life tariff did not breach Article 3 at the imposition of the sentence. They argued that the possibility of review in a whole-life tariff would offer the offender illusory, potentially false, hope. The offer of such hope, the Government argued, is something which Article 3 does not require.

25.3 The Government argued from the historic case *R v Bieber* [2008] EWCA Crim 1601 in which it was held that a whole-life term should not be considered irreducible and cited the Secretary of State's power to release a whole-life prisoner on compassionate grounds, under section 30 of the Crime (Sentences) Act 1997, as evidence that a whole-life tariff given in the UK is reducible.

25.4   When questioned about the lack of a 25-year review, the Government said the aim of the 2003 legislation (which as stated removed this power from the Secretary of State) was to 'judicialise' sentence reviews. Schedule 21 of the 2003 Act provides sufficient sentencing guidelines for judges effectively to choose tariffs for a life sentence. They also reiterated that all three applicants' tariffs were imposed by judges[49] and all were subject to a review in the Court of Appeal.

25.5   The applicants submitted that their tariffs were in fact irreducible because no prisoner had been released under section 30 of the 1997 Act or any other power. They also disagreed with the chamber's finding that a whole-life tariff was not contrary to Article 3 when it was issued. The applicants submitted that for a prisoner to be incarcerated for the remainder of his or her life upon sufficient grounds would not breach Article 3 but being kept incarcerated purely for the purpose of punishment would be a breach. At the point of sentence the sufficiency of ongoing grounds for incarceration cannot be judged and thus a whole-life tariff with no real prospect of review would be a breach of Article 3 from the outset. The applicants argued that throughout a whole-life tariff the justification of the sentence (deterrence, public protection, etc.) may change and that a review must be in place to ensure there are still sufficient grounds to justify incarceration for life.

26.   The Grand Chamber's finding

26.1   In its judgment the Grand Chamber drew a distinction between the work of the court in interpreting the European Convention on Human Rights and the role of member states in determining penal policy.

26.2   It was accepted that, in principle, decisions on sentence reviews and release arrangements fall outside the scope of the court provided the member states' systems do not contravene rights in the convention. Nor would the court assume the role of deciding appropriate sentence lengths; accepting that states must be free to impose whole-life tariffs on those who have committed the most serious crimes.

---

49.   Some critics of this European ruling which liberal commentators saw as a victory for human rights described the Strasbourg court as having 'a warped moral compass': see, e.g. http://thejusticegap.com/2013/07/whole-life-term-ruling-warping-of-moral-compass/

26.3   The judges reaffirmed two points decided in *Kafkaris v Cyprus* App. No. 21906/04 (ECHR, 2008):

   (a)   A life sentence does not become irreducible by the fact in practice it may be served in full, and no issues arise under Article 3 if a life sentence is in fact, and in law, reducible;

   (b)   In determining whether a life sentence is irreducible, the court must ascertain whether a prisoner has a prospect of release.

   Therefore, for a life sentence to be compatible with Article 3 it must be capable of being reviewed and there must be a prospect for the prisoner of release.

26.4   The Grand Chamber declined to comment on when a sentence review should take place. This is at the discretion of the member state. Reviews are necessary in order to ensure that a prisoner remains incarcerated on legitimate penological grounds, though the court accepted these grounds may change throughout the duration of the sentence.

27. Developments post-*Vinter*

27.1   *R v McLoughlin* was heard in the Court of Appeal on 24 January 2014. The court was specially constituted to hear three applications for permission to appeal a whole-life term following the decision in *Vinter*. The court considered the whole-life sentence of Ian McLoughlin, who was convicted of murdering Graham Buck by stabbing him in the neck when he came to the aid of a neighbour who McLoughlin was robbing.

27.2   The Court of Appeal considered *Vinter* and came to the following conclusions:

   (a)   It did not read the judgment of the Grand Chamber in that case as in any way casting doubt on the fact that there are crimes that are so heinous that just punishment may require imprisonment for life; and

   (b)   It considered the ruling that an irreducible whole-life sentence was not compatible with Article 3 of the convention, and found that the regime established by Parliament did provide for reducibility. This was because section 30 of the Crime (Sentences) Act 1997 allows for the Secretary of State to release a life prisoner on licence if he or she is satisfied that exceptional circumstances exist which justify the prisoner's release on compassionate grounds.

27.3 The court concluded that in the case of *McLoughlin* the seriousness was exceptionally high and just punishment required a whole-life order. The fixed minimum term of 40 years given by the previous judge, who misunderstood the law and believed he was not able to give a whole-life sentence, was for that reason unduly lenient. The court therefore quashed the minimum term of 40 years and made a whole-life order.

28. Summary of *Harkins v UK* (as it pertains to whole-life sentences)

28.1 Phillip Harkins was arrested in the UK in 2000 for the murder of Joshua Hayes, who was killed in Jacksonville, Florida, by being shot in the head during a robbery. The government of the USA requested that Harkins be extradited, stating that the maximum sentence he risked in that country was life imprisonment.

28.2 In 2007, Harkins appealed to the European Court of Human Rights, arguing that a sentence of life imprisonment without parole would constitute a breach of Article 3. He submitted that his sentence would be irreducible as, in Florida, executive clemency was the only avenue by which he could seek reduction of his sentence and that the procedure for seeking such a reduction was subject to minimal procedural protections.

28.3 The case of *Harkins and Edwards v UK* [50] was heard by a chamber of seven judges. On 17 January 2012, the chamber held unanimously that a mandatory life sentence without possibility of parole is not *per se* incompatible with the convention.[51] It considered that an Article 3 issue would arise if it could be shown that continued

---

50. App. Nos. 9146/07 and 32650/07 [2012] ECHR 45.

51. On the same date, a chamber of the European Court of Human Rights also gave judgment in *Vinter and Others v The United Kingdom*, App. Nos. 66069/09, 130/10 and 3896/10 [2012] ECHR 61. The applicants in both *Vinter* and *Harkins* requested referral to the Grand Chamber. The request was granted in *Vinter*, but rejected in *Harkins*. Consequently, the judgment in *Harkins* became final on 9 July 2012.

incarceration no longer served any legitimate penological purpose and that the sentence is *de facto* and *de jure* irreducible. The chamber found the applicant had not shown that his incarceration would not serve any legitimate penological purpose and considered the possibility of executive clemency under Florida State law meant the sentence was theoretically reducible in accordance with the principles in *Kafkaris v Cyprus*[52] (where only a bare possibility of release was sufficient).

28.4 On 11 November 2014, Harkins submitted a further appeal to the European Court of Human Rights. He argued that the decision in *Vinter* (subsequently applied in the context of an extradition to the USA in *Trabelsi v Belgium*[53]) makes it clear that it is not compatible with Article 3 to expose a defendant to a whole-life sentence in the absence of certain minimum procedural and substantive safeguards. In essence, three things are required: firstly, a proper review mechanism; secondly, objective pre-established review criteria that are accessible to the prisoner; and finally, a purposive review to ascertain 'whether, while serving his sentence, the prisoner has changed and progressed to such an extent that continued detention can no longer be justified on legitimate penological grounds'.[54] Harkins submitted that the present complaint was not 'substantially the same' as that made in his previous application as the injustice complained of was different and would occur in a different legal landscape. He also argued that the Grand Chamber further confirmed the position of *Vinter* in *Murray v The Netherlands*.[55]

28.5 In *Trabelsi*, the European Court found that a 'mere' possibility in the reduction of a sentence through substantial cooperation or compelling humanitarian reasons, or by a presidential pardon, did not satisfy the test in *Vinter*. Similarly for Harkins, the Florida State system puts the power of granting early release from a whole-life sentence entirely in the hands of the State Governor, who has unfettered discretion, and there is no right to a substantive review at any specified point. Additionally, the Governor is under no requirement to consider the progress of the prisoner and his or her rehabilitation and there are no criteria that govern the commutation of

---

52. App. No. 21906/04 [2008] ECHR 143.
53. App. No. 140/10 [2014] ECHR 893.
54. Ibid, para 137.
55. App. No. 10511/10 [2016] ECHR 408.

a sentence. The applicant submitted that these aspects of Florida State law directly contradict the requirements laid down in *Vinter, Trabelsi* and *Murray*.

28.6 Harkins also submitted that a whole-life sentence is a violation of Article 6 (right to a fair trial), as it gives no opportunity for the court to consider the facts of the individual offence and offender and constitutes a flagrant denial of justice involving a total exclusion of judicial control over the determination of the proportionate sentence in the individual case.

28.7 In June 2017, the Grand Chamber declared the complaints lodged by Harkins inadmissible. It held that the applicant's Article 3 complaints were substantially the same as those already examined by the European Court in 2012 in *Harkins and Edwards*. It considered that subsequent case law does not constitute 'relevant new information' within the meaning of the admissibility criteria under Article 35 of the convention. The Grand Chamber held that the 'Court's case-law is constantly evolving and if these jurisprudential developments were to permit unsuccessful applicants to reintroduce their complaints, final judgments would continually be called into question by the lodging of fresh applications'.[56]

28.8 The Grand Chamber likewise dismissed the complaints raised under Article 6 of the convention. In particular, it held that 'there is no evidence to suggest that the trial court would be anything other than "independent and impartial"; that the applicant would be denied legal representation; that there would be any disregard for the rights of the defence; that there would be any reliance on statements obtained as a result of torture; or that on other grounds the applicant would risk suffering a fundamental breach of fair trial principles'.[57]

29. The continuing use of the whole-life sentence in England and Wales

29.1 European jurisprudence in respect of the whole-life tariff in England and Wales clearly allows for its continuing use (and with a lukewarm approach to review).

---

56. *Harkins v The United Kingdom* App. No. 71537/14 (15 June 2017), para 56.
57. Ibid, para 66.

29.2 In order to impose a whole-life sentence which is Article 3 compatible English judges and the Secretary of State must not impose an irreducible sentence and must institute review dates. The ongoing reasons in favour of incarceration may change over the course of such a sentence and punishment for its own sake may legitimately form a part of a member state's approach to sentencing those prisoners convicted of the most serious crimes committed against another person.

29.3 It is clear that the European Court of Human Rights may temper the use of the whole-life tariff in England and Wales but it by no means precludes it, nor does the situation post-*Vinter* appear to have been substantially altered by that and later decisions.

30. *Vinter* — 'A misunderstanding of English law' in any event?

30.1 There is a body of thought that would advocate that *Vinter* revealed a misunderstanding of English Law. It is therefore necessary for the purposes of this paper to briefly review the history of the whole-life sentence; the definition of which some would argue has been somewhat confused over time.

30.2 The death penalty for murder was suspended in 1965 and abolished in 1969. A sentence of mandatory life imprisonment was substituted, which meant the offender's loss of liberty during his lifetime, subject to the Home Secretary's prerogative power to discharge the prisoner from custody, at any time, on the condition that there was no further risk to life or limb. If a prisoner were to be released on licence he or she could be recalled to prison at any time to serve the rest of his or her indefinite sentence.

30.3 It is within the meaning of the mandatory life sentence that much confusion lies. Society has come to understand that such imprisonment was akin to the American punishment of life without the possibility of parole. This is where the misunderstanding lies. The alternative penalty of a mandatory life sentence was in fact intended to be a curtailment of liberty, not necessarily custodial.

30.4 Academics who staunchly oppose the whole-life sentence have argued that a myth has been harnessed, to persistently political ends, to suggest that there was established in

1965 life imprisonment as involving a custodial sentence for the period of the whole of the prisoner's natural life.

30.5 It is surely a great cause for concern that a person could be incarcerated for the duration of their life on the basis of a misunderstanding of the sentence that can be rightfully imposed.

30.6 It would not be argued that *Vinter* was a misapplication of the European Convention on Human Rights. However, it is of great concern that the whole-life sentence which the Grand Chamber was adjudicating on is conceptually quite different to the mandatory life sentence introduced following the abolition of the death penalty in 1965. This is yet another example of confusion within the law of murder that is yet to be clarified.

Conclusion

31.   Our views summarised

31.1   *Modernising Justice* continues to strongly disagree with comments received from Michael Gove and Sir Oliver Heald QC, which indicate that there is no reason to consider further reform of the law of murder. The law of murder is based on a definition formulated in the seventeenth-century, a time when accepted punishments included having body parts removed for committing theft. The law surrounding this definition has of course advanced since then, but *Modernising Justice* submits that, in light of the case law discussed in this paper, the passing of over a decade since the last review of the law in this area is a matter for deep concern.

31.2   The lessons we should learn from the cases of *Gnango* (2011), *Vinter* (2013), *McLoughlin* (2014), *Jogee* (2016) and *Harkins* (2017) are as follows:

  (a)   The rules determining the application of accessory liability need to be restated. Judges have been unable to provide decisive guidelines as to how such rules should be applied, resulting in inconsistency, confusion, and ultimately misapplication of the law.

  (b)   The law surrounding murder as a whole needs to be clearer. It is, in our view, not acceptable for cases to be incorrectly prosecuted for 30 years because of a misunderstanding and misapplication of the law, and this is an issue that must not be ignored. A reform of the whole system of homicide offences could prevent such an extensive miscarriage of justice reoccurring.

  (c)   The admissibility of public policy considerations needs to be determined. Convictions must be made purely on an application of the law, not on the basis of 'mob mentality'.

  (d)   The system of whole-life imprisonment needs to be reviewed. In our view, the Court of Appeal has erred in holding that our current system does not breach Article 3 of the European Convention on Human Rights in light of the European Court of Human Right's judgment in *Vinter*. There should be a clear definition of what constitutes a 'prospect of release', which in our view should be more than the Secretary of State's authority to release a life prisoner on licence, on 'compassionate grounds', if 'exceptional circumstances' exist—the bar is too high. *Modernising Justice* would further point out that the judgment in *Harkins,* where the risk of a life sentence without parole except in the most miniscule of circumstances, if at all, was no bar to extradition to another jurisdiction, compounds matters in that the court declined to apply the advances made in *Vinter* and *Trabelsi* and reconsider the case in light of these developments.

31.3　*Modernising Justice* proposes that an independent committee be convened to review the law of homicide, with the objective of re-framing the law in such a way that it avoids the injustices which have been witnessed in the last decade's case law and to bring the UK's approach in line with a modern way of thinking. *Modernising Justice* proposes that an independent committee be convened to review the law of homicide, with the objective of re-framing the law in such a way that it avoids the injustices which have been witnessed in the last decade's case law and to bring the UK's approach in line with a modern way of thinking. This committee, importantly, should be made up of lay people who have experience of working in the administration of justice in some capacity, as well as a small number of lawyers to take on a solely advisory role.

About Modernising Justice

Modernising Justice was created in 2004 as the Homicide Review Advisory Group (HomRAG), for the purpose of running alongside the work of the Law Commission as it reviewed aspects of the law on murder. It was set up on the initiative of Sir Louis Blom-Cooper QC and the late Professor Terence Morris, and initially chaired by the late Very Reverend Colin Slee, Dean of Southwark. In essence, the group is concerned with promoting a just law of murder.

In 2011, HomRAG published its first report, 'Public Opinion and the Penalty for Murder: Report of the Homicide Review Advisory Group on the Mandatory Sentence of Life Imprisonment for Murder'. The report was targeted at law-makers and other interested parties, and focused on the unjust and outdated nature of the mandatory life sentence for murder.

HomRAG rebranded as *Modernising Justice* in 2016, and is currently chaired by Sir Louis Blom-Cooper QC. Since 2011, it has tracked a number of important and high-profile developments in the law relating to murder and whole-life sentences. The group continues to believe that the law of homicide is outdated and in desperate need of reform.

Current membership: Sir Louis Blom-Cooper QC (Chair), Sir Robin Auld PC, Bryan Gibson, John Harding CBE, Malcolm Dean, Colin Colston, Josepha Jacobson, Nigel Pascoe QC, Victoria Ellis, Michael Charalambous (Co-secretary), Andrew Wheelhouse (Co-secretary).

Contact: modernisingjustice@gmail.com

Appendix: Correspondence

1. **Letter to the Rt Hon the Lord Chancellor and Secretary of State for Justice, Michael Gove MP, dated 9 October 2015.**

Dear Lord Chancellor

Reform of the Law of Murder

By way of an introduction, we are Modernising Justice—a multi-disciplinary group concerned with the just application of the criminal law and its processes, established in 2004 as HomRAG (Homicide Review Advisory Group) under the chairmanship of the late Canon Colin Slee. Historically, the group has had a particular focus on the promotion of a just law of murder and its penalty. For reference, we have attached a copy of the report issued by the group in 2011 which dealt with public opinion on murder and manslaughter and was widely accepted.[58]

We have continued to express our support for the content of your recent speech of 23 June 2015 to the Legatum Institute, and our sincere gratitude for your recognition of those very serious issues. We felt it the ideal opportunity to share with you two suggestions which we strongly believe would bolster the 'one nation justice policy' of which you spoke.

Underpinning a modern criminal justice system must be a stronger legislative regime. Modernising Justice is deeply concerned that the law of murder has not been the subject of genuine scrutiny since the Law Commission ten years ago, whose recommendations have not been implemented. It is high time and of the utmost importance that this is addressed. The group would therefore ask that this issue be firmly placed on the Government's agenda.

In making the pledge to address the law of murder Modernising Justice would welcome the establishment by you of a departmental committee with a two-year time limit. We would advise that this committee be made up of legal professionals and individuals from other professional fields and other walks of life. The law of murder is a vital social and moral issue, as is the linked issue of culpable homicide. As such, the make-up of the committee must reflect that.

Finally, may we once again express our deepest support for the aims and aspirations expressed within your speech. Modernising Justice looks forward to supporting the Government in its aspirations to establish a justice system that works 'for everyone in this country'.

Sincerely yours,

Sir Louis Blom-Cooper QC

For and on behalf of Modernising Justice

---

58. See *Public Opinion and the Penalty for Murder: Report of the Homicide Review Advisory Group on the Mandatory Sentence of Life Imprisonment for Murder* (2011), Waterside Press.

2. Reply by Michael Gove to Modernising Justice dated 31 October 2015

Dear Sir Louis

Reform of the Law of Murder

Thank you for your letter of 9 October in which you outline the work of Modernising Justice and your warm [words] about my speech at the Legatum Institute. I was very interested to read about the work of the group.

I note your suggestion that I set up a Departmental Committee to undertake a further review of the law of murder. As you know, the Government carefully considered the Law Commission's 2006 Report on Murder, Manslaughter and Infanticide. As a consequence, a reformed partial defence of diminished responsibility was enacted in the Coroners and Justice Act 2009. At the same time the defence of provocation was replaced with a new, modernised, partial defence of loss of control.

The Coalition Government then took the view that there were no grounds for revising the formulation or operation of the partial defence or taking forward a more substantial review of the law of homicide. I believe those were the right decision, and the Government has no current plans to review the law on homicide.

Successive Governments have held the view that the retention of the mandatory life sentence for murder is an essential part of the law's recognition of the seriousness of this gravest of crimes. The law therefore continues to provide a mandatory life sentence for murder and a maximum penalty of a life sentence for manslaughter. Sentencing in individual cases is entirely a matter for the Courts, taking into account all the circumstances of the offence and the offender. The Court will consider all relevant circumstances when determining whether to impose a life sentence for manslaughter and, if so, the appropriate minimum term. The Court will also take into account the principles set out in statute which apply to sentencing for murder. I am therefore not persuaded that there is a need to review the mandatory life sentence.

Thank you for writing to me and I appreciate your continued interest in the law in this area.

Yours

Michael Gove

3. Further letter to Michael Gove, Lord Chancellor dated 2 February 2016

Dear Lord Chancellor

Reform of the Law of Murder

Thank you for your letter of 31 October.

Modernising Justice has carefully considered your letter, the contents of which have given our group much cause for reflection.

We respectfully disagree that there were no grounds for taking forward a more substantial review of the law on homicide. In 2005, the Law Commission were instructed on very narrow terms of reference and, as such, were unable to review many tenets of the law of murder that are unsatisfactory.

In order to make our case, Modernising Justice intends to produce an academic paper noting the developments of the law of murder to date and how the law, as it currently stands, is unacceptable.

As you will be aware from your research, the reform of the law of murder is a subject about which our group feels very deeply. With that in mind, we will return to this point.

Sincerely yours,

Sir Louis Blom-Cooper QC
For and on behalf of Modernising Justice

4. Letter from Modernising Justice to the Rt Hon Elizabeth Truss MP, Lord Chancellor and Secretary of State for Justice dated 23 January 2017

Dear Justice Secretary,

Reform of the Law of Murder

I write to you on behalf of Modernising Justice, a group of individuals from various disciplines who are concerned with ensuring the fairness of our criminal justice system. The group was established in 2004 as the Homicide Review Advisory Group (HomRAG) under the chairmanship of the late Dean Colin Slee. Our particular focus, currently and historically, has been on how the law of murder and sentencing could be reformed. We published a report on this topic in 2011,[59] which was widely accepted, and will be publishing a second report in early 2017. We have enclosed the 2011 report for your reference.

We wrote to your predecessor Michael Gove in October 2015, to express our concerns that the law of murder had not been the subject of genuine scrutiny since the Law Commission's review ten years previously, whose recommendations had not (and still have not) been implemented. We requested of him that this issue be firmly placed on the Government's agenda, and that a departmental committee be established to address this issue. Mr Gove's response indicated that he did not agree that there was a need to reform the law of murder at that time. This correspondence is also enclosed for your reference.

As the new Secretary of State for Justice, we present to you the same concerns, and ask whether you are open to the prospect of revisiting this important issue. We suggest that this is particularly important in light of the recent case of *R v Jogee* [2016] UKSC 8.

We look forward to hearing your thoughts on this matter, and would be very grateful if you could respond as soon as possible.

Sincerely yours,

Sir Louis Blom-Cooper QC

Assenting members: Robin Auld, Bryan Gibson, John Harding, Malcolm Dean, Colin Colston, Josepha Jacobson, Nigel Pascoe, Victoria Ellis, Rachel Norman and Jack Michaels.

---

59. See previous footnote.

5. Reply to Modernising Justice received from the Right Honourable Sir Oliver Heald QC MP, Minister of State for Justice dated 27th February 2017

Dear Sir Louis

Thank you for your letter of 23 January 2017 on behalf of Modernising Justice in which you ask whether the Government will consider reforming the law of homicide, particularly in the light of *R v Jogee*.

The Government places great importance on this area of the law, particularly to ensure that the legislative framework reflects the seriousness of these offences and that public confidence in the law is maintained. As you may know, in September last year, I gave evidence to the Justice Select Committee who were considering whether there was a need to reform the law of homicide, in particular whether the framework should be restructured, replacing murder and manslaughter with a three tier structure of 'first' and 'second' degree murder and manslaughter, as recommended by the Law Commission in 2006.

As I made clear in my evidence to the Committee, and at subsequent times, I do not share the view that the law of homicide is in urgent need of reform. The law of homicide covers all the relevant areas of criminality and there are, as far as the Government is aware, no immediate legislative gaps which need to be filled. In addition, I have to say that at least in the last few years, there has been very little demand from the public for a review of the law of homicide.

Moreover, the Law Commission's proposal to reform the law of homicide is not the only proposal. Even among supporters of a 'three tier structure', there is no clear consensus about where the boundaries should be drawn. You, I believe, take a different approach favouring a single homicide offence with no mandatory life sentence. On the other side of the argument, there is likely to be public concern about any proposed changes to the categories of homicide which could appear to dilute the seriousness of, or affect the sentence in, any particular case.

More specifically on *Jogee*, the Justice Secretary wrote to the Justice Select Committee in November 2016, concluding that no review of the law of homicide would be necessary as a result of that judgement. The Court's decision only alters the law in relation to cases involving parasitic accessory liability. It does not purport to have an impact on the wider law of joint enterprise. Neither does the judgement mean that everybody convicted on the basis of parasitic accessory liability will have their convictions quashed. The Court made it clear that a convicted offender would have to make an out-of-time application to the Court of Appeal or seek a review by the Criminal Cases Review Commission. The judgement confirms that the Court of Appeal would only grant permission to appeal if it considered the applicant had suffered 'substantial injustice' and that 'it will not do so simply because the law applied has been declared to have been mistaken'. The Court states that the same principles would govern the decision of the Criminal Cases Review Commission if asked to consider referring a conviction to the Court of Appeal.

The Government has considered the implications of the *Jogee* judgement extremely carefully and we are particularly mindful of the uncertainty that the judgement created for victims' families who do not know if the offenders involved in the death of their loved ones would successfully appeal. The judgement will, however, only apply to a narrow category of cases and the Government has agreed that families will be kept informed by the relevant agencies if a prisoner successfully appeals or is released from custody.

Therefore, the Government has no current plans to review the law of homicide generally or as a result of the *Jogee* judgement.

Yours sincerely

Sir Oliver Heald QC MP

6. Letter from Modernising Justice to the Rt Hon David Lidington MP, Lord Chancellor and Secretary of State for Justice dated 4th January 2018

Dear Justice Secretary,[60]

Reform of the Law of Murder

I write to you on behalf of Modernising Justice, a group of individuals from various disciplines who are concerned with ensuring the fairness of our criminal justice system. The group was established in 2004 as the Homicide Review Advisory Group (HomRAG) under the chairmanship of the late Dean Colin Slee. Our particular focus, currently and historically, has been on how the law of murder and sentencing could be reformed. We published a report on this topic in 2011, which was widely accepted, and will be publishing a second report in early 2018. We have enclosed the 2011 report for your reference. Currently, the group is also concerned with road traffic killing, and the Ministry of Justice's plans to increase the maximum sentence for causing death by dangerous or careless driving from 14 years to life.

As Secretary of State for Justice, we present to you our concerns, and ask whether you are open to the prospect of revisiting this very important issue, which continues to engage the interest and concern of all sections of the legal profession and the public.

We invite you to meet with Modernising Justice, to discuss our proposals in more detail.

We look forward to hearing your thoughts on this matter, and would be very grateful if you could respond as soon as possible. Our email address for correspondence is modernisingjustice@gmail.com.

Sincerely yours,

Sir Louis Blom-Cooper QC

For and on behalf of Modernising Justice

Assenting members: Robin Auld, Bryan Gibson, John Harding, Malcolm Dean. Colin Colston, Josepha Jacobson, Nigel Pascoe, Victoria Ellis, Michael Charalambous, Andrew Wheelhouse.

Cc: Dominic Raab MP

---

60. As this pamphlet was going to press there was a further change of Ministers, when a letter in similar terms was sent by *Modernising Justice* to the new Lord Chancellor and Justice Secretary, David Gauke MP.

CPSIA information can be obtained
at www.ICGtesting.com
Printed in the USA
BVHW02s1053210318
511100BV00021B/43/P